5.15

£3.00

D0364048

BRISTOL CITY LIBRARIES
WITHDRAWN AND OFFERED FOR SALE
SOLD AS SEEN

Renew by phone or online
0845 0020 777

Joss Stone

mind body & soul

This publication is not authorised for sale
in the United States of America and / or Canada

Wise Publications
part of The Music Sales Group
London / New York / Paris / Sydney / Copenhagen / Berlin / Madrid / Tokyo

Bristol Library Service

AN 2883105 5

Published by
Wise Publications,
8/9 Frith Street, London, W1D 3JB, England.

Exclusive Distributors:
Music Sales Limited
Distribution Centre, Newmarket Road,
Bury St Edmunds, Suffolk, IP33 3YB, England.

Music Sales Pty Limited
120 Rothschild Avenue, Rosebery,
NSW 2018, Australia.

Order No. AM91753
ISBN 0-7119-3891-1
This book © Copyright 2004 by Wise Publications.

Unauthorised reproduction of any part of this
publication by any means including photocopying
is an infringement of copyright.

Music arranged by Paul Honey.
Music processed by Paul Ewers Music Design.

Printed & bound in the United Kingdom.

www.musicsales.com

BRISTOL CITY COUNCIL
LIBRARY SERVICE
Class
No.
M 5
Alloc. AL   Suppl MR

Your Guarantee of Quality:

As publishers, we strive to produce every book
to the highest commercial standards.

While endeavouring to retain the original running
order of the recorded album, the book has been
carefully designed to minimise awkward page turns
and to make playing from it a real pleasure.

Particular care has been given to specifying
acid-free, neutral-sized paper made from pulps which
have not been elemental chlorine bleached.

This pulp is from farmed sustainable forests
and was produced with special regard for the
environment.

Throughout, the printing and binding have been
planned to ensure a sturdy, attractive publication
which should give years of enjoyment.

If your copy fails to meet our high standards,
please inform us and we will gladly replace it.

Right To Be Wrong

Words & Music by Desmond Child, Joss Stone & Betty Wright

© Copyright 2004 BMG Music Publishing Limited (33.34%)/Copyright Control (66.66%).
All Rights Reserved. International Copyright Secured.

I'm step-ping out_____ in-to the great un - known,_____

I'm feel-ing wings___though I've nev-er flown.

Got a mind_____ of my

own,

I'm flesh and blood_____

to the bone, I'm not made of stone.

Got a right_____ to be

11

whatever's out there waiting for me, I'm gonna face it willingly.

Mm.

Got a right to be

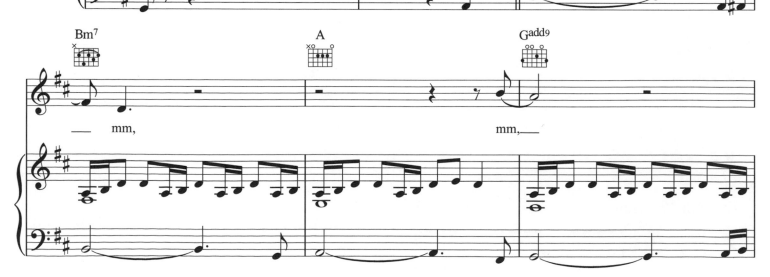

so just leave me alone. Mm,

mm, mm,

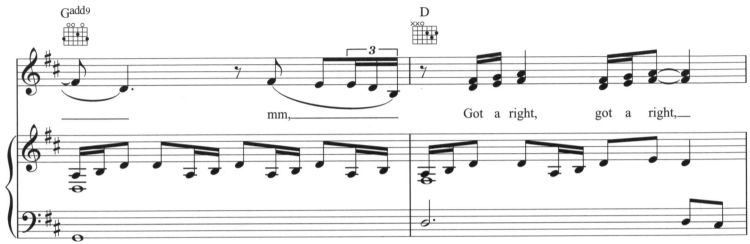

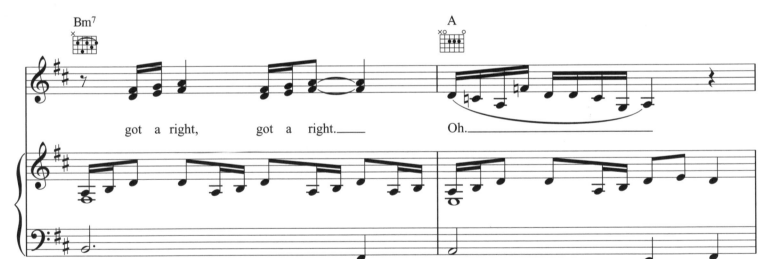

Jet Lag

Words & Music by Jonathan Shorten, Conner Reeves & Joss Stone

© Copyright 2003 BMG Music Publishing Limited (33.33%)/
Universal Music Publishing Limited (33.33%)/Rondor Music (London) Limited (33.34%).
All Rights Reserved. International Copyright Secured.

16

jet lag,— jet lag. Ba-by don't you know you real-ly, real-ly got it go-in' on. Hmm.

Ba-by don't you know you real-ly, real-ly got it go-in' on. Yeah, yeah.—

Ba-by don't you know you real-ly, real-ly got it go-in' on.—

Ba-by don't you know you real-ly, real-ly got it go-in' on.

18

E♭m11
B♭m9
Jet lag and I nev - er ev - en left the ground, see it's
like that ev - 'ry time you come a - round. Ooh I'm so hung -
- ov - er and I ne - ver ev - en touched a drop,
G♭9
Repeat and fade
jet lag, jet lag.

You Had Me

Words & Music by Francis White, Joss Stone, Betty Wright & W. Stoker

© Copyright 2003 BMG Music Publishing Limited (35%)/
Universal Music Publishing Limited (35%)/Copyright Control (30%).
All Rights Reserved. International Copyright Secured.

no - bo - dy got___ no bus - 'ness___

stress - ing all___ the time.___ Tak-ing it back,_ I'm tak - ing it back,

tak-ing back_ my life._____ I've seen it_____ be - fore; I'm

tak - ing back___ my life.___ N.C.

Spoiled

Words & Music by Lamont Dozier, Joss Stone & Beau Dozier

© Copyright 2004 BMG Music Publishing Limited (33.34%)/Copyright Control (66.66%).
All Rights Reserved. International Copyright Secured.

now I don't know what I left you for._____ See, I thought that I could re-place you,

he can't love me the way you do._____ Till now I nev-er knew ba-by. I'm

spoiled by your love, boy, no mat-ter how I try to change my mind,

what's the point, it's just a waste of time. I'm spoiled by your touch, boy, the

To Coda ⊕

love you give is just too hard to fight, don't want to live with-out you in my life, I'm

spoiled.

Mmm.

2. I tried to tell my-self that I'd be ov-er you in a week or two,

but ba-by, that was 'bout a year_ a-go._ I've nev-er seen the word *love* so per-

Less Is More

Words & Music by Jonathan Shorten, Connor Reeves & Joss Stone

♩ = 76 (swung semiquavers)

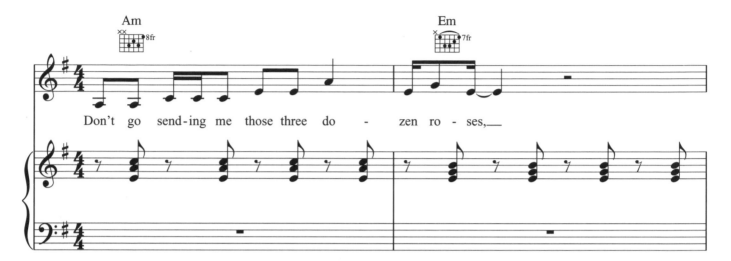

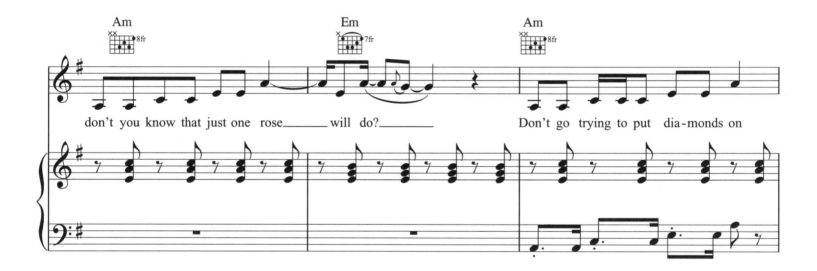

© Copyright 2002 BMG Music Publishing Limited (33.34%)/
Universal Music Publishing Limited (33.33%)/Rondor Music (London) Limited (33.33%).
All Rights Reserved. International Copyright Secured.

34

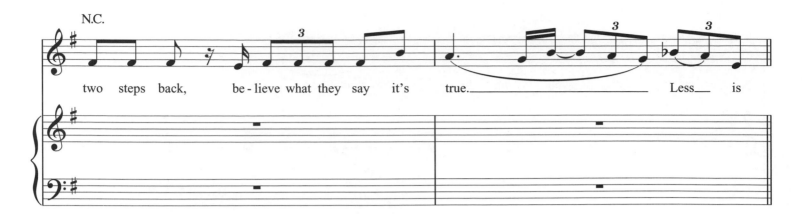

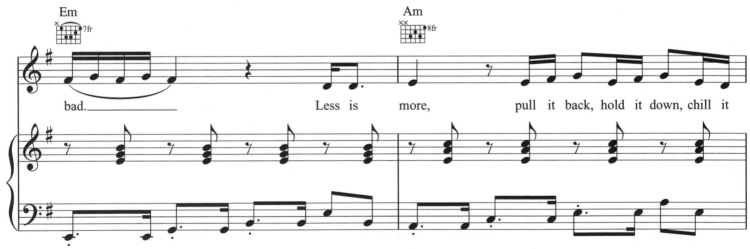

Give me a chance___ to miss you, boy, I don't mean___ to diss you but,

I tell you I need___ some space_ and still you call me up three times___ a day._ You know_

___ ba-by, you're crowd-ing me out,_ have-n't you heard___ less is more?___

Repeat and fade

___ Less is more,___ lis-ten me boy.___ Less is

39

Don't Cha Wanna Ride

Words & Music by Desmond Child, Steve Greenberg,
Eugene Record, Michael Mangini, Joss Stone, Betty Wright & William Sanders

♩ = 68   **Swung semiquavers**

© Copyright 2004 Copyright Control (81.67%)/EMI Music Publishing Limited (18.33%).
Copyright Control (81.67%)/EMI Music Publishing Limited (18.33%).
All Rights Reserved. International Copyright Secured.

feel like   you just___ might   be some-one who I could get in - to.   But I
girls say   you're hard to please,   but I think that I got just what you need.   Get your

nev - er   seem to catch___ your eye,   and it's been bug - gin' me why I ev - en try,   still, you're
face out   of the mir - ror,   then___ may - be you could con - si - der   this___

some - one I'd like to get___ to know,   is there room for me in your one - man   show?
girl who's knock - in' right at___ your door   make room for me in your one - man   show.

A   car this fine   don't pass your___ way   ev - 'ry day,___   don't___

43

you, do__ you, do__ you, do__ you know__ that they__ can't give__ you what__ I__

give?____ No Lord.____ Ooh.____

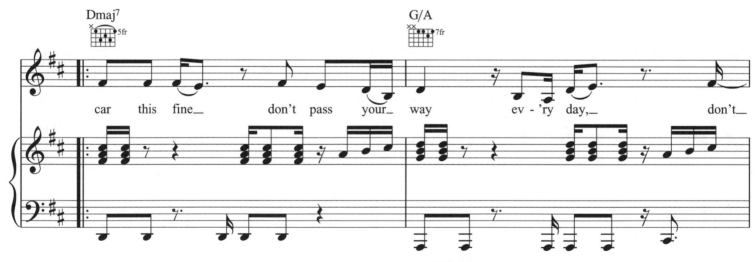

car this fine__ don't pass your__ way ev-'ry day,__ don't__

__ cha wan-na ride__ ba - by?

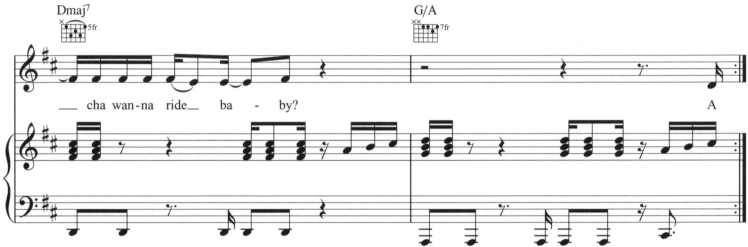

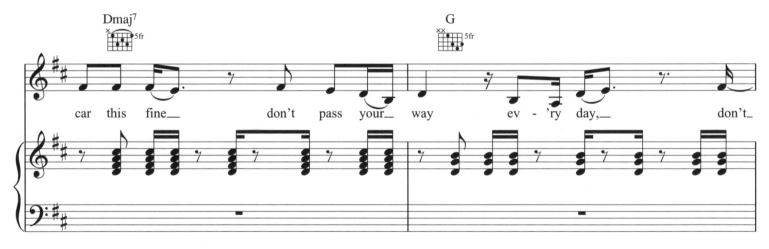

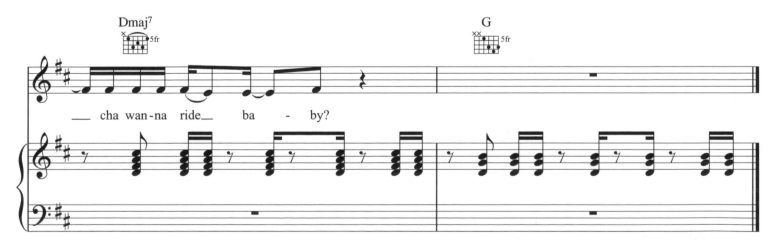

Young At Heart

Words & Music by Joss Stone & Salaam Gibbs

© Copyright 2004 BMG Music Publishing Limited (50%)/EMI Music Publishing Limited (50%).
All Rights Reserved. International Copyright Secured.

You're wast-ing____ your time____ trying to tear us up a - part, you can't stop____ our plans

____ we were des-tined from the start. He loves me____ I love_ him, and ev-en though we're young at

1.

heart,_____ see you're the one in de-ni - al. 2. My

2.

you're the one in de-ni - al._____

You're the one in de-ni - al,_____

49

You're wast-ing___ your time___ trying to tear us up a - part, you can't stop___ our plans___

___ we were des-tined from the start. He loves me___ I love___ him,___ and ev-en though we're young at

heart,_____ see you're the one in de-ni - al. you're the one,___ you're the one.___

Repeat and fade

You're the one in de-ni - al._____

51

Snakes And Ladders

Words & Music by Jonathan Shorten, Connor Reeves & Joss Stone

© Copyright 2003 BMG Music Publishing Limited (33.33%)/
Universal Music Publishing Limited (33.33%)/Rondor Music (London) Limited (33.34%).
All Rights Reserved. International Copyright Secured.

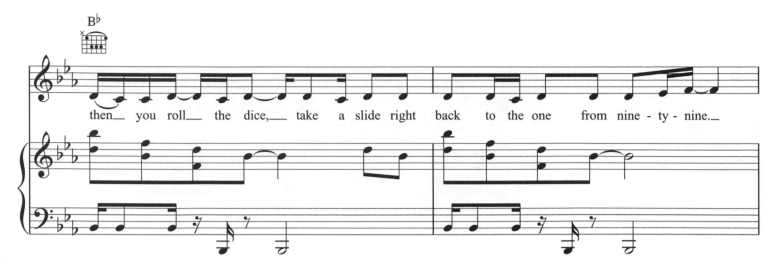

then__ you roll__ the dice,__ take a slide right back to the one from nine - ty - nine.__

Is it gon-na go on__ like this__ for-ev-er, are we gon-na take that__ last step__ to-ge-ther?

Go - ing 'round and 'round and up and down feels just like Snakes And Lad-ders.

1.

N.C.

La la la la la la la la la la la la la, 2. Ba - by

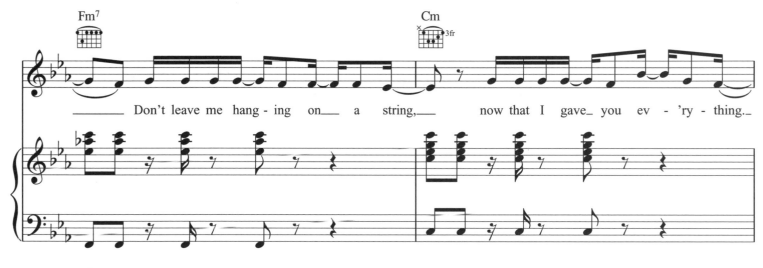

What's the name of the game_ that we_ are play-ing? But when-ev-er I think_ that we_ are win-ning,

then_ you roll_ the dice,_ take a slide right back to the one from nine-ty-nine._

Is it gon-na go on_ like this_ for-ev-er, are we gon-na take that_ last step_ to-ge-ther?

1.

Go - ing 'round and 'round and up and down feels just like Snakes And Lad-ders.

feels just like Snakes And Lad-ders. la la la la la la la la

la la la la la, la la la la la la la la la la

la la la la la, la la la la la la la la la la la la la, la

la la la la la la la la la la la la.

Understand

Words & Music by Steve Greenberg, Michael Mangini, Joss Stone,
Betty Wright & Angelof Morris

© Copyright 2004 BMG Music Publishing Limited (20%)/
EMI Music Publishing Limited (20%)/Copyright Control (60%).
All Rights Reserved. International Copyright Secured.

you.____ Do__ you un - der - stand that I'm in love__ with you? I keep__ our

song ____ on re - peat,____ on__ my i - Pod____ ev - en when I

sleep.____ And in my dream____ I'm hold - ing you,____ a - lone__ on an is-

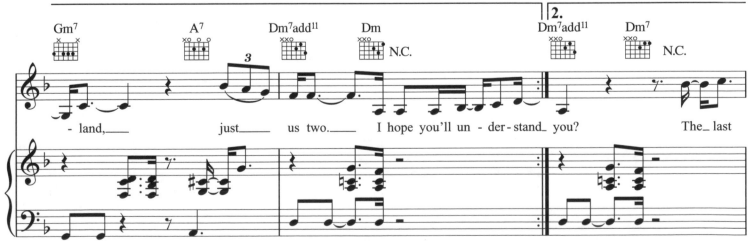

- land,____ just____ us two.____ I hope you'll un - der - stand__ you? The__ last

59

guy_____ had me__ so wrong,_____ he kept__com - plain-ing I was a - way__ too__

long. Don't treat me_____ that__way, 'cause in___ your head___ you've got__ to

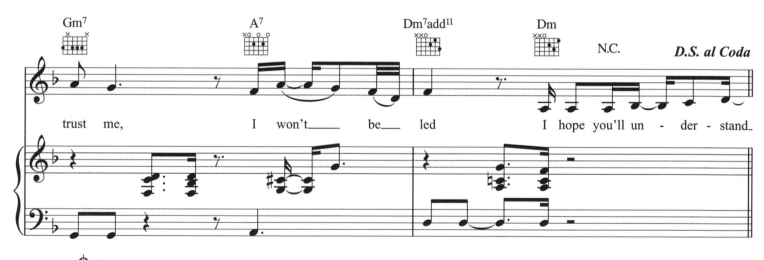

trust me, I won't____ be__ led I hope you'll un - der - stand__

D.S. al Coda

Coda

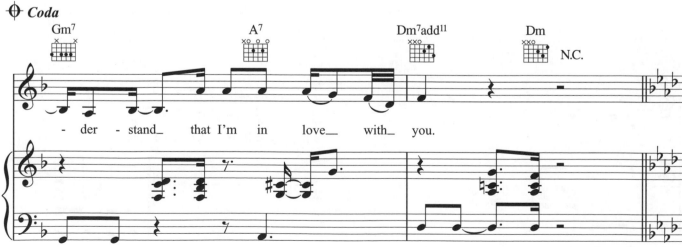

- der - stand__ that I'm in love__ with__ you.

I hope your mind___ ain't work-ing ov-er time,___ I hope your me-mories are

full of good times_ with me._____ Don't_ trip if_ right now___ I can't_

___ ans - wer_ the phone,_ 'cause you know that_ soon_ I'll be_ com-ing

home._____ I hope you'll un - der-stand_____ that I_ can't____ al - ways_

Security

Words & Music by Steve Greenberg, Daniel Pierre & Joss Stone

© Copyright 2003 BMG Music Publishing Limited (33.33%)/EMI Music Publishing Limited (66.67%).
All Rights Reserved. International Copyright Secured.

On an-y clock up-on the wall___ the time___ is al - ways now,___

so ba - by kiss the past good-bye,___ don't let the fu - ture blow your mind.___

Just sit back and chill,___ take things___ as they___ come,___ you

can't be a-fraid to live for to - day,___ I will be with you each step of the way. If your

70

Don't Know How

Words & Music by Jeremy Ruzumna, Daniel Pierre,
Justin Gray & Curtis Richardson

1. You caught my eye and out of no-where you ap-
2. Got so much time, your at-ti-tude, ev-'ry-thing,

-peared by sur-prise, and it's not like me but cer-tain-ly
you make me smile, think I'm not fall-ing in deep for no reason

© Copyright 2004 EMI Music Publishing Limited (50%)/Copyright Control (50%).
All Rights Reserved. International Copyright Secured.

Boy__ you're so fine,__ and I want to tell you so, I'm__ much too shy,__

wan - na__ make you mine,__ but__ I don't__ know how.__

__ Aah.__

Feel - in' cra - zy,__ my heart - beat's rac - ing now, I__ can't fight it,__

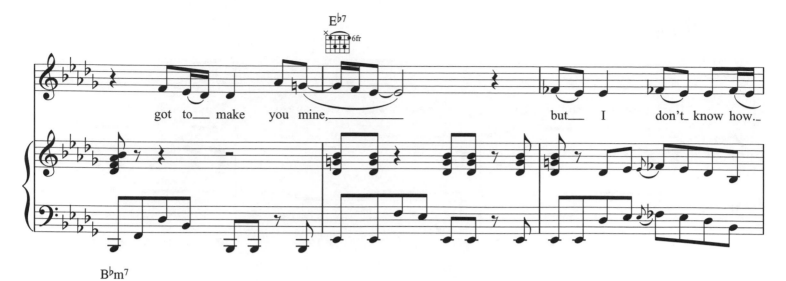

got to___ make   you   mine,_____   but___ I   don't_ know how.__

___   Yeah,   yeah,_____   yeah,___   oh._____

Ba - by___   let   me   know what's   up   now,___   you got   to   show me

some - how___   how you feel,   'cause I   can't   take   it   no_____

more.

I real-ly need to know what's good with you boy.

D.S. al Coda

Coda

Mm,

mm, mm, mm, mm, mm.

Repeat and fade

Ooh.

Killing Time

Words & Music by Beth Gibbons, Joss Stone & Betty Wright

1. May-be life__ is bet-ter off__ this way,__
2. I have tried to put it from__ my mind,__

but what a-bout the o-thers who aren't__ here__ to-day?
to bu-ry all the trou-bles that are__ left__ be-hind.

© Copyright 2004 BMG Music Publishing Limited (7.5%)/Chrysalis Music Limited (90%)/Copyright Control (2.5%).
All Rights Reserved. International Copyright Secured.

80

yeah.__ *Guitar solo ad lib.*

Play 3 times

Stop what you're do - ing be -

-fore you do it all wrong a - gain.__ You will have to get it right__ this time.

poco rall.

Be-fore it gets all out of hand.__

Torn And Tattered

Words & Music by Andy Dean, Benjamin Wolf,
Betty Wright & Austin Howard

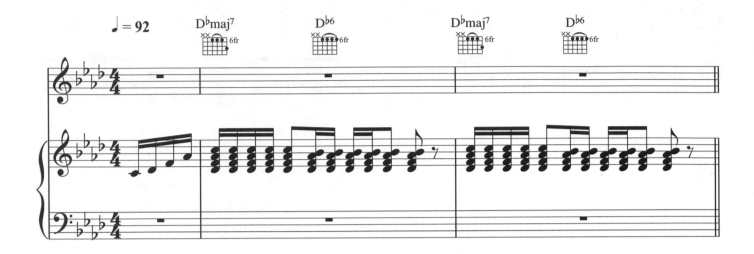

© Copyright 1993 Big Life Music Limited (45%)/Universal Music Publishing Limited (50%)/Copyright Control (5%).
All Rights Reserved. International Copyright Secured.

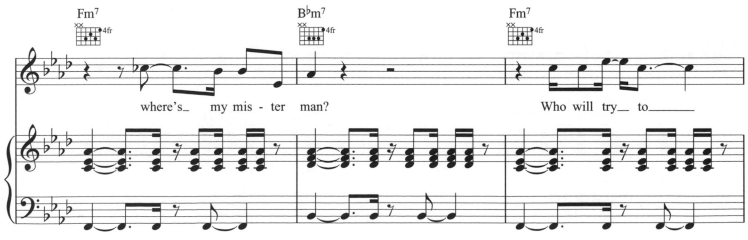

de-ny_ me now_ ev - 'ry - thing_ I plan_ to be._

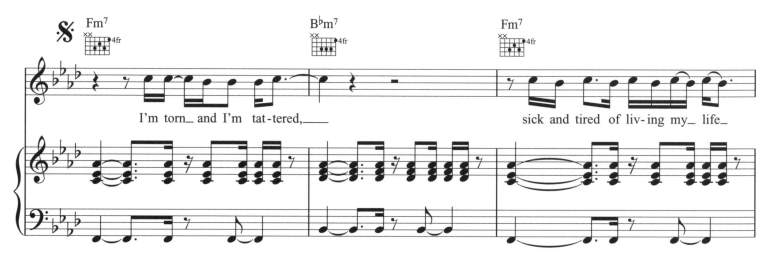

I'm torn_ and I'm tat-tered,_ sick and tired of liv-ing my_ life_

sing-ing the same_ old song. Oh I, I feel_ a lit-tle bat-tered,

looks like I'm liv-ing my life_ run-ning a one - man show._ Oh,_____

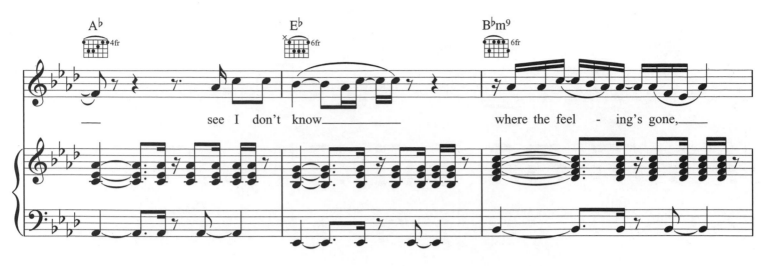

see I don't know_____ where the feel - ing's gone,_____

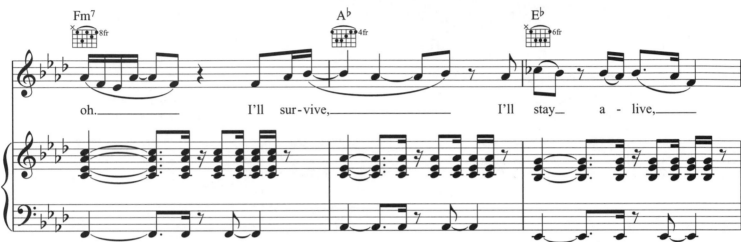

oh._____ I'll sur - vive,_____ I'll stay_ a - live,_____

To Coda ⊕

and you know_ I'll car - ry on, on,_____ on, Oh.

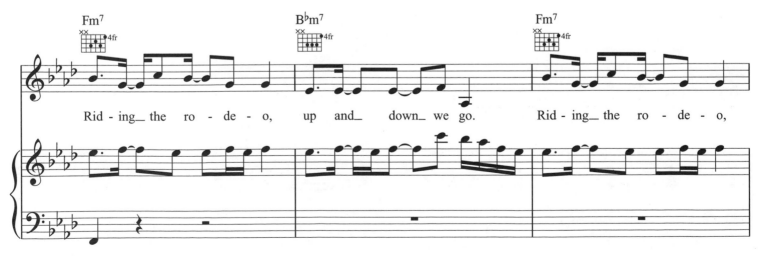

Rid - ing_ the ro - de - o, up and_ down_ we go. Rid - ing_ the ro - de - o,

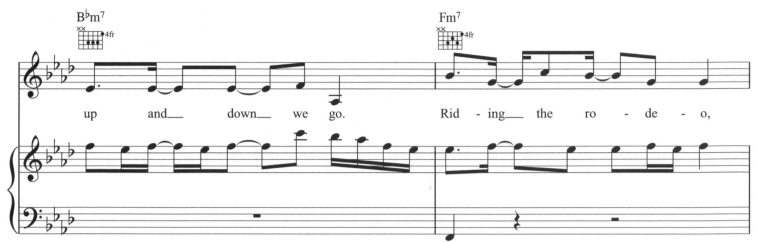

up and down we go.   Rid - ing the ro - de - o,

D.S. al Coda

up and down we go.   Rid - ing the ro - de - o,   (I don't know).

Coda

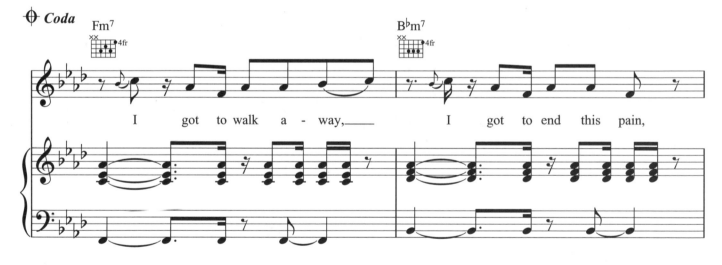

I   got to walk a - way,___   I   got to end this pain,

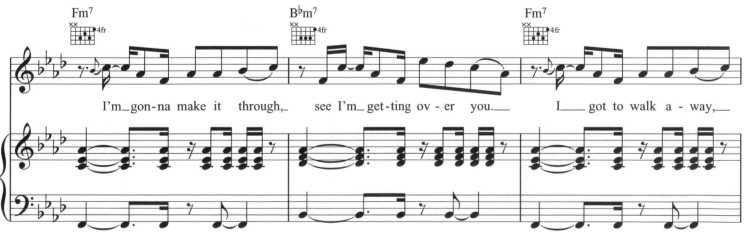

I'm_gon-na make it through,_   see I'm_get-ting ov - er you.___   I___ got to walk a - way,___

87

I___ got to end this pain, I'm_ gon-na make it through,_ I'm_ get-ting ov-er you.

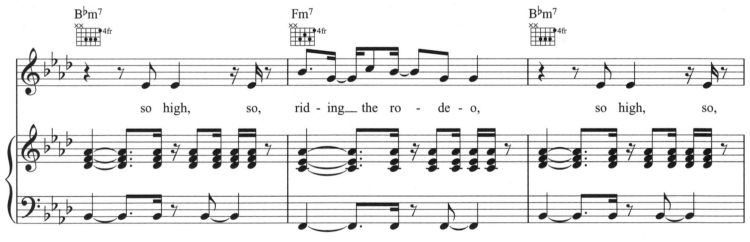

Rid-ing__ the ro - de - o, so high, so, rid-ing__ the ro - de - o,

so high, so, rid-ing__ the ro - de - o, so high, so,

rid-ing__ the ro - de - o, (I don't know). I'm torn_ and I'm tat-tered.

Sleep Like A Child

Words & Music by Patrick Seymour

To-night__ when the dark-ness comes,__ why don't we treat it like a friend?__ Then we'll both be glad__ to see the night, and we'll be

© Copyright Universal Music Publishing Limited.
All Rights Reserved. International Copyright Secured.

Repeat and fade

123456789